SHIFT

HOW TO DEAL WHEN LIFE CHANGES

ABIGAIL BRENNER, MD

ISBN: 1453636943
ISBN-13: 9781453636947
LCCN: 2010909007

To Bronwen, Georgia,
Isabella, and India

ACKNOWLEDGMENTS

Thanks to family and friends who are a constant source of encouragement and support.

With gratitude to those who took the time out of their busy lives to read, comment, and offer valuable insights—Rita Battat Silverman, Monique Guffey, Dr. Christine Ranck, and Helen Adrienne.

I especially want to thank Louise Gikow for her sharp mind, amazing way with words, sense of humor, and vision. It was Louise who convinced me that this book was important enough to stand on its own.

CONTENTS

INTRODUCTION
WHY *SHIFT* NOW?

You never change things by fighting the existing reality. To change something, build a new model that makes the existing model obsolete.
Richard Buckminster Fuller

These are times of incredible change and radical transition. The world today has shifted beyond anything expected, predicted, or imagined. The legacy of 9/11, the war in Iraq, the recent economic meltdown, and unemployment crisis have sent shock waves through virtually all of our lives. These events have dramatically changed the way we perceive the world and ourselves in it. It is safe to say that we can no longer be so sure about the stability and continuity of institutions that have sustained our existence for so long.

It should come as no surprise that many major personal life changes happen very suddenly in these times as well. Career changes have to be made almost instantly when an industry goes belly up. People can lose their homes within a few months of losing their jobs. There is a great need to understand change and transition in an increasingly changing world. Frightening as this is in the wake of an uncertain future, the good news is that we can now refocus our attention on the one and only thing of which we *can* be certain—ourselves. *SHIFT* is needed *now*, to help people navigate the world as it is *now*.

Technology is a constantly changing force in our lives, providing access to an unfathomable amount of information. Few of us could have comprehended the rapidity of change we all experience on a minute-by-minute basis, or the effects this barrage of information and unfiltered stimulation has upon us. We are simultaneously empowered and overwhelmed by the easy access and availability of information. Somehow, the way the Internet has leveled the playing field (making us all instant experts) has left us also feeling that we should be able to control life. But instead, when our life does shift, we often find ourselves bewildered and insecure.

The rapid shifts in Pop culture profoundly affect us as well, changing us both at the conscious and unconscious levels. Reality shows give us a voyeuristic view of people's lives that can make us feel inadequate in our own lives, leaving us unclear about our own authentic paths. The cult of celebrity figures prominently in our lives, penetrating our consciousness and insinuating itself into our sense of self. A byproduct of this phenomenon is the epidemic striving for physical perfection and for the consumer-driven pursuit of "having it all." With so many supposed ways to be happy and satisfied, how are we to navigate the way that is right for us as individuals? *SHIFT* addresses the radical measures people are often forced to make in today's world.

As a practicing psychiatrist for many years, I've watched far too many individuals randomly wandering through their lives, unfocused and out of touch with where they've been, and almost clueless about where they're going. They simply had no game plan for life, no *roadmap* for the journey. So you can imagine how complex things really become when the problem of personal disconnection from one's own individual life is compounded by the onslaught of external stimuli, constantly bombarding and assaulting us with too much, and often disturbing, information from the world stage.

Many of us are poorly equipped to cope with and effectively process all that is happening around us. Yes, we're surviving, but we don't have the basic necessary tools to adapt to change and thrive in the process. Simply put, we need to find a way to take back responsibility for ourselves, in essence, to shift the way we think about how we want to be in the world.

Transitions are not just meant to be endured, but rather to be welcomed and embraced with anticipation and excitement for the potentials they tap into and for the unlimited possibilities they make available to us. One of my chief missions in life is to help people make better transitions. To that end, my goal is to address universal themes of change and transition, those to which most of us can readily relate, and to provide a contemporary model for transition as well as the necessary tools to help make the journey through life both satisfying and purpose-filled. In other words, I want to give you a *road map*, something you can refer to for guidance and assistance as you move from transition to transition. Ultimately, it is our cumulative transitions that become our life.

Aside from the idea provided by the definition, of moving, transferring, altering, or changing direction, position, place, or form, *SHIFT* implies the ability to provide for one's own needs. Beyond the meaning for the individual though, *SHIFT* refers to a qualitative change, a quantum leap toward transformation for all of us. The "life program" most of us have already in place by the time we are very young includes limiting beliefs and attitudes about change. *SHIFT* is an invitation to transcend that, to embrace change as an opportunity to explore, not only what lies beyond our familiar reach, but also the possibilities and untapped potentials waiting for us, and to push our perspective outward toward new frontiers of thought and consciousness.

There are substantial benefits to be gained from this new way of thinking. For one thing, when we become reliant upon ourselves for our own further advancement, we become responsible for our own personal evolution. A better understanding of who you are and who you are not allows for the personal discernment and critical scrutiny that helps you separate what is important for you personally, apart from the dictates of your society. You no longer have to settle for following along with the pack. For certain, this gives you a fair amount of control for what you choose to do in a changing world.

Mastering the process of *SHIFT* is an empowering tool for growth and development. The provocative and engaging exercises are designed to challenge your beliefs and uncover your limitations. Ultimately, you will be able to make decisions and move forward on your own path, flexible to life's ebb and flow, rather than remaining fixed to a script containing outdated ideas and beliefs that no longer serve you personally and all of us, collectively. *SHIFT* offers a practical, yet inspirational way to confront change in an increasingly changeable world and provides a dynamic approach to navigating these changes.

PART ONE: CHANGE

Life happens; and what happens is something called change. Change may come from within ourselves as we develop and grow psychologically and emotionally, or through encounters with significant others—our family, friends, colleagues, and intimates. These changes may be self-generated, within our control and design, or cast upon us by fate from seemingly out of the blue. They may be subtle and gradual, easy and welcomed, or difficult and demanding. We may meet change with acceptance and grace, or with vehement protest and resistance.

The personal significance of each change occurs when we decide to *make* change. This means we move from the passive state of just watching how things unfold to taking some action that enables us to utilize the change to create an outcome of our own choice. Shifting our focus from what happens (the events themselves) to what we do with what happens is another way to describe transition. Ultimately, the way we *make* change is our choice and personal responsibility.

Part One presents an overview of the many faces of change, its nature, as well as the accompanying emotions and responses to it. This review is an essential piece for understanding how *SHIFT* works, for while the nature of change may be the same as it's always been, the world in which we live certainly is not.

THE NATURE OF CHANGE

> *Life is a series of natural and spontaneous changes. Don't resist them—that only creates sorrow. Let reality be reality. Let things flow naturally forward in whatever way they like.*
> **Lao Tzu**

Change happens. What we do with what happens to us, how we utilize it for our personal progress and evolution, is the essence of transition. The danger of going through change without allowing ourselves to transition through it is that true change may not actually occur. In *The Way of Transition*, author and leading expert on transition, William Bridges states that some people even "make changes so they won't have to make transitions." If we are too uncomfortable to stay the course through transition, too anxious to fix the problem, we may lose the message and its accompanying transformative effect. Change without transition, then, may only serve to recreate old scenarios and reinforce old patterns of behavior. Before change can have a lasting effect on us, can transform who we are and what happens to us, we must allow it to wash over and through us, cleansing and purging the old, baptizing us with a renewed sense of self and purpose.

Change is a shift in a given life situation. Some changes are the result of biology and the passage of time, within the natural cycle or order. Other changes happen as a result of circumstance or fate, a proverbial "date with destiny." Still others are self-generated, under our own control and willful effort. Our experiences are externally or internally focused; they either follow a linear pattern, regulated by chronological time, space, and the social structure, or transcend ordinary time and emerge from the depths of our psyches and our own internal strivings.

Everything changes all the time, so the ancient philosophers and mystics tell us. The *I Ching, the Book of Changes*, is a classic Chinese text that has served as a tool for decision-making and for predicting the future for well over five thousand years. Although everything is transient, continuously changing, the concept of change and its evolving process adhere to basic natural laws, which by their cyclic and repetitive properties make change essentially unchanging. The *I Ching* is comprised of a system of symbols whose purpose is to help us find order within the random occurrences of life.

Lao Tzu said, "Easy gives rise to difficult...resonance harmonizes sound...after follows before." Ideally, every situation in life cycles through six mutable, yet predictable stages that are mirrored within each symbol of the *I Ching*: coming into being, beginning, expanding, moving toward the highest potential, achieving peak potential, and descending toward the opposite. The ancients recognized that all life follows the rhythm of the universe. It is the wise person who internalizes this rhythm, harmonizes with the "surrounding All," and conforms what he does to the flow of life, the *Tao*.

So often we try to live through our changes without experiencing them.

Julia Cameron

While change may insinuate itself, interrupting the usual flow of our daily lives and disrupting our normal functioning, it certainly affords us the opportunity, and the challenge, to examine our lives and to alter the course, if we so choose, or stay our course, making better choices and decisions. The only thing change really asks of us is to give it a chance. Turning too quickly away from what it offers may deprive us of receiving much needed information, taking certain action, or being gifted by a powerful lesson. *The key here is to understand that change is the rule, not the exception.* When we have accepted and mastered that concept, it's far easier to adapt our lives to it with the knowledge and trust that we are being carried in its flow.

Our human existence depends upon the interaction of three organizational systems: the body (soma), the psychic (psyche), and the communal or social (ethos). Ideally, healthy personality development is determined by the complementary interplay of all three. When this fails to occur, any breach within the workings of the essential organizing processes may result in "somatic tension, individual anxiety, or social panic," according to developmental psychologist and psychoanalyst, Erik Erickson.

Erickson's pivotal theory of the eight psychosocial crises in the life cycle forms the basis for understanding how healthy psychosocial development effectively engages each new life stage and its accompanying developmental task or crisis. Each of these crises is a turning point and should not be viewed as threatening or catastrophic, even though it may seem that way. Although one may feel incredibly vulnerable during any of these crucial periods, in actuality it is a fertile time of heightened potential. How an individual embraces and resolves the conflict or crisis in any given stage impacts, either positively or negatively, whether the individual masters conflicts and crises moving forward. A sense of mastery of each stage and its associated crisis produces ego strength, or ego quality. *Even when an individual fails to complete a given task, carrying it unfinished into future stages, each subsequent stage provides added resources and opportunities to resolve old conflicts and crises.*

Here is a summary of the stages, and the psychosocial crises and ego qualities that accompany each stage of the life cycle, according to Erickson:

Infancy:	Trust vs. Mistrust:	HOPE
Early Childhood:	Autonomy vs. shame, doubt:	WILL
Play Age:	Initiative vs. guilt:	PURPOSE
School Age:	Industry vs. inferiority:	COMPETENCE
Adolescence:	Identity vs. Identity confusion:	FIDELITY
Young Adulthood:	Intimacy vs. isolation:	LOVE
Maturity:	Generativity vs. self-absorption:	CARE
Old Age:	Integrity vs. despair, disgust:	WISDOM

Most notable in each stage is the pairing of competing elements. According to Erickson, the ego-syntonic (meaning that thoughts, impulses, attitudes, and behaviors are acceptable to one's self-conception) element "supports growth and expansion, offers goals, celebrates self-respect, and commitment of the very finest" while the ego-dystonic describes elements which are dissonant and challenging to us. For Erickson, "conflict and tension are sources of growth, strength, and commitment." Ultimately, how an individual resolves these basic conflicts greatly influences and deeply impacts not only the emerging personality, but also the growth and evolution of the whole individual.

When change and transition are superimposed upon this organizing principle of human development, things really get interesting, and complicated. Erickson's work helps illuminate and clarify how an individual meets and processes intrinsic change and, by inference, may help predict whether or not an individual is able to rise to the task of making transition.

EMOTIONS OF CHANGE

In any moment of decision the best thing you can do is the right thing, the next best thing is the wrong thing, and the worst thing you can do is nothing.

Theodore Roosevelt

The emotions accompanying change can run the gamut from excitement to dread depending on the individual's anticipation and level of expectation. However, the process of movement from change through transition can be broken down into easily recognizable sequential stages—loss, uncertainty, discomfort, insight, understanding, and integration—which are fairly predictable. Each of these stages is accompanied by very specific emotions.

Take a moment now and think about a major change in your life. Even when a change has long been anticipated, a sense of giving something up or letting something go may feel like a loss. Without the familiar and habitual to rely upon, you may feel cut off and out of control.

The uncertainty generated by this process may leave you doubting yourself. Questions may arise as to whether it's better to make the change, or to stay with what you already know. A disconnection from who you once were may leave you feeling undecided and skeptical. An uncertainty about the truth may lead to disbelief.

Discomfort can manifest as distress, uneasiness, and/or anxiety. The *critical zone,* between discomfort and insight, is the place of decision about what is to ultimately happen—either move on to the next stage and discover new possibilities, or retreat in fear. With insight, there is a breakthrough; something is revealed that offers direction. This is very encouraging, for what had been strange and unfamiliar is beginning to take on a recognizable form.

Understanding what the change has brought you eventually leads to integration. At this final stage, you are able to incorporate what you have learned, including the new capacities and strategies that you can call upon in the future.

Having a sense of what to expect along the way, even in general terms, and having a name to call it, may be just good enough to keep you moving in the right direction. In fact, the decision to move on through insight and integration restores control, bringing with it a feeling of hope in a new beginning.

Just a word about change when it is unexpected and imminent: When you know change is coming, you have time to prepare yourself. Even then, it's often frightening and provocative. With sudden changes, such as those happening through traumatic or catastrophic event, you are at the mercy of the event and the immediate necessary steps that must be taken. You may not be able to process what is happening to you until well after the event/situation has stabilized. Eventually, though, it's important to make the effort to understand the change, the transition through it, and the meaning it holds for your life.

Exercise: The Loss Timeline

Loss is a big deal in our culture. In fact, the idea of loss probably accounts for many of humanity's woes. We are conditioned to *have* and to *achieve*, whether this is expressed in the accumulation of material wealth, or through personal accomplishments. There is nothing inherently wrong about wanting and achieving. That is, until we start spending an inordinate amount of time worried and anxious about how to safeguard what we have. And when our self-esteem and personal status/identity is measured largely by what we have and achieve, you can understand how the loss of anything dear to us can carry substantial consequences. (The joke goes that when you play a country/western song in reverse, you get back everything you lost! Were it that simple.)

Loss can mean anything—death, a finished relationship, divorce, illness, a physical move, loss of a job, change in status or identity (even a good change), or part of the natural cycling through change. Construct a chart of events/happenings that signify loss to you. Choose any time frame you like, for example, dividing the timeline into decades, or quarters. List the losses, rating them by depth and intensity, either using words (mild, moderate, severe, extreme), or dots (1 to 5). In columns next to each event/happening note your emotions, then your feelings, then your behavior.

Now answer these questions:

- How long did it take you to process each event?
- Did you successfully process each loss, meaning did you find a satisfactory solution or resolution?
- If not, how did that loss carry over into your life?
- What patterns are emerging about the way you deal with loss?
- What beliefs do you hold about loss? Are these carry-overs from your earliest experiences with loss? If so, are these beliefs as applicable today as they were long ago?
- Are you able to discover something new about yourself through this exploration into past loss?

Answering these questions will hopefully give you a better understanding of your relationship to loss. The answers may provide important clues to help you understand why resistance to change may be operative in your life.

RESPONDING TO CHANGE

Each man is questioned by life; and he can only answer to life by answering for his own life; to life he can only respond by being responsible.

Victor Frankl

Why do some people thrive through change and transition while others experience great difficulty? Are there individual characteristics or traits that explain how people weather the storm of change? Is there a personality profile that describes better coping skills and contributes to a better outcome?

The answer is that there's not a simple answer. As we've seen, being initially responsive to change and being curious and open to the possibilities it offers are essential. The level of mastery of each successive psychosocial stage and the accompanying developmental task/crisis is an important determining factor as well.

Certainly, having mastered the art of change over the course of a lifetime provides a great advantage. The more experience you have with the process, the more you come to know what to expect along the way. More importantly, you gain knowledge through your own personal history through transition of your response to change. Over time, you have the opportunity to shift how you respond to change in order to create a more satisfying experience.

In addition, being able to step back and observe the singular change/transition within "the bigger picture" helps to moderate how we think and feel about a certain event. When all is said and done, a singular event may not seem as sweeping and dramatic if placed in this context. Learning to keep things in proper perspective may help reduce distraction and mitigate emotional responses, keeping us solidly focused in "the here and now" of our lives. And as you may guess, the "usual suspects" help enormously: persistence, patience, resilience, personal motivation, optimism, balance, humor, and a healthy sense of self and purpose.

Some research has suggested that adapting an orientation to life that relies primarily on one's own personal resources, rather than on the "externals" (relationships, work, etc.) that define life for many of us, is advantageous for making change. When dependency on outside forces is diminished, it becomes easier for the individual to reinvent him or herself whenever necessary.

I've observed both in my practice and in life that so much of what we do is *reactionary*. We are constantly responding and reacting to what is imposed upon us from outside of ourselves, rather than just being able to take the necessary *action* in accordance with what is most essential for our well-being. Since many of our problems/issues have been "inherited" from our parents, passed down through the family, and even generationally driven, much of our time is spent trying to distance, disengage, and disentangle ourselves from these. Sometimes there is a conscious recognition that these issues are being superimposed on our lives, but other times these issues only get expressed by subconsciously acting them out in our relationships with others. This might lead you to ask, "Whose neurosis is this, anyway?"—a really good question.

Imagine how much easier life would be if we could really clean up our own "emotional act," get clear about our own heartfelt feeling, and respond in a way that feels authentic to us and makes us proud of ourselves. Think how much better a world it would be if children were initially *programmed* in a healthier way that readily promoted their own development and growth. This is why identifying and learning how to access our own core beliefs is so essential.

People often enter therapy at the crossroads of change, as the individual seeks to understand the change and what it implies—its impact, its meaning. Sometimes the insights sought are in response to some external event. The change "out there" requires a corresponding shift "in here." Sometimes, however, the change is a drive from within. This internal push is the evolution of personal consciousness. What had once been fulfilling no longer works for the individual. The developmental process toward transformation eventually moves through dissatisfaction and conflict with the status quo through a heightened awareness about one's condition or situation, finally to a place of opening to new possibilities and potentials.

In *The Heart and Soul of Change: What Works in Therapy* researchers sought to find what was effective in the various modalities of treatment (more than 200) and techniques associated with these models (more than 400) that define available psychotherapy approaches. Their research found little evidence to recommend one modality/technique over another. Instead, they focused their attention on the common elements of all of these models and techniques.

The researchers identified four factors responsible for change in therapy. Surprisingly, the model/technique of therapy itself accounted for only 15 percent of improvement. The placebo effect, the patient/client's expectation and hope for what would happen accounted for another 15 percent of success during therapy. The main element responsible for change was the client/extra-therapeutic factor, which accounted for 40 percent of improvement. It is the client's/patient's desire to change that allows him or her to draw upon his/her own "generative, self-healing capacities" that drive the success of the treatment. The relationship factor, the therapeutic alliance with the therapist, accounted for 30 percent of success. Whether this was due to a "corrective emotional experience," the development of new capacities and strategies, the reinforcement of healthy adaptive behaviors, or the therapist's empathic stance is yet unclear.

Change happens when the patient/client takes responsibility for making change happen. In summary, there is no one way, one method, or one technique that is better or more effective than any other. Having said that, *SHIFT* is not a model or technique, but rather a process, a way of thinking based on the evolutionary unfolding of consciousness.

TRANSITIONS

When I let go of what I am,
I become what I might be.
Lao Tzu

Transition is an internal process that informs us that it's time to move on, that we are ready and committed to leave behind old behaviors and patterns. This ability to let go strongly suggests our volitional control over what happens to us as opposed to just letting things happen of their own accord. What we leave behind may be an old identity or status, if we're talking about social change, or perhaps an outdated part of our self that is no longer in sync with our developing personality and emerging persona, if we mean psychological change. An anticipated ending, and certainly one we have initiated, may be dealt with more smoothly and with less angst than an ending that surprises or shocks us by its sudden appearance and dramatic presentation.

The unexamined life is not worth living.

Socrates

As part of the process through transition, we shed an old identity—who we've thought we were up until the change. Essentially, the energy that has powered an outdated role, status, or persona needs to be released in order for it to be available for what we are to become. This process may leave us wondering, "If I am not who I once thought I was, then who am I?" A real sense of loss for *what once was* may accompany this process.

For transition to do its magic as the process unfolds, we have to begin to question what we once called our *reality*. For most of us, what is *real* is fixed and absolute. We are invested in believing that what we experience is incapable of being changed, probably because we feel reassured and safe when life continues on in the same way it always has. But reality is, in fact, illusive. As we let go of the people and events to which we've been attached, we also let go of a thinking that has imbued these specific people and events with special significance and meaning. This is the process of stripping away the veil of idealism surrounding the world we've created for our own purposes, in order to reveal things as they truly are. So in the process of shifting our focus, shifting our consciousness begins.

Before we can find and anchor ourselves to something new, we must go through a period of not knowing. We may know we are moving forward but we don't know yet where we're going. Beyond the difficulties experienced in transition is the promise inherent in the rite of passage; we move forward into the unknown in a simple, yet deeply profound act of faith and trust that we will be led to where we need to go. If *making change* is to be effective, the initiate, the hero, must undergo a death and rebirth. This process includes a disintegration, or a taking apart (without falling apart), and a reintegration, a putting together, of the pieces of the new *changed* self.

In this transitional place, we have the opportunity to turn back, but not to return, to view what once was with a perspective altered by time and distance; we can see all that was for what it is, rather than for what we wished it had been. Each *re-view* broadens our perspective on our life; the cumulative effect of this is learned wisdom.

Oddly enough, the place of not knowing, where we don't know how to belong because we are between identities, is also the place of our greatest authenticity. When all is stripped away from the identity that is "you," the realization may hit that what you refer to as *my life* is just simply the core of who you are, your "real" self, wrapped in the "stuff of life," all of the external things that make up life as we think about it. When these are peeled away layer by layer, what is left is all that really matters—*who you are*. When people say, "This is just who I am" as if it were written in stone, what needs to be added is, this is who I am *given the set of circumstances*. Given totally different conditions, who knows who *you* would be.

Exercise: The Life Timeline

This is a *re-view* of significant life events/experiences. Create a timeline beginning from your earliest memory. Move forward, perhaps demarcating your timeline by decades or periods of your life.

- What events were pivotal in your life?
- How did these events impact you?
- Choose the one most pivotal event in your life, either positive or negative. Why does this event stand out most for you?
- How did positive experiences catapult you forward, supporting your growth and development?
- How did negative experiences inhibit you, preventing healthy development, keeping you stuck in thinking and/or believing in a certain way?

Exercise: Track your Emotions/Feelings

Identify the single most important emotion—for example, happiness, sadness, anger, hurt, jealousy, and so on—attached to each of the major events you've indicated on your timeline. Try to remember what feelings you expressed around each of these events. Become aware of the quality of these feelings—how strong they were, their duration, their power over you, how distracting or disruptive they were to you.

- Did your feelings accurately and authentically express what emotion was linked to each event?

- If not, were you acting out what you thought or believed was expected of you?
- What is the quality of your feeling(s) around each of those events from the perspective of today?

LIFE CYCLES

Whatever begins, also ends.
Seneca

Events in our lives happen in a sequence in time, but in their significance to ourselves they find their own order: the continuous thread of revelation.

Eudora Welty

Although it may be easier to visualize your life unfolding through time in a linear fashion, as we did in the life timeline exercise, it's ultimately important to understand the cyclic nature of your transitions. The outcome of any major event/experience will certainly carry consequences moving forward. If you've learned from your experiences, then your choices as you move through your life should better support you and your goals.

If you haven't learned the lessons from your experiences, you may once again find yourself struggling to achieve a specific desired outcome. What are the repetitive patterns of your life cycling around over and over again? What have you learned about yourself each time you've cycled through each repetitive pattern?

Sometimes it's the actual outcome that provides valuable feedback, important insights that help us understand and put in perspective the meaning of the event/experience itself. In other words, the wisdom gained by successfully mastering the experience can help shed light on the origin and nature of the experience itself. We are able to see it in a new light.

Exercise: Life Themes

We all have life themes, a specific issue or two that dominates our life. Sometimes this central theme defines our life purpose or mission; sometimes it is about our greatest pain. For some, it is the driving force of their life, for others, their nemesis. Tracking major life transitions will probably reveal the theme(s) that keeps coming up over and over again—difficult relationships, authority, money, power, abandonment, deprivation, the consequences of low self-esteem, to name just a few.

- What is your life theme(s)?
- How has this theme affected the way you are in the world?
- How much of a role does this theme play in the way you define yourself?
- Does this theme allow you to express yourself in a way that feels affirming and supportive of who you are?

- Does this theme negatively influence you? What do you get out of staying in this mode?
- If this theme is a result of limiting beliefs, what would be the outcome if you could let those go?
- How does this theme influence or define your life's mission or purpose?

Exercise: Life Lessons

T.S. Eliot said, *"Everyone gets the experience; some get the lesson."* Everything we do in life has the potential to be a life lesson. For each stage of life, there are specific lessons to be mastered. Remember Erickson's psycho-social tasks, or crises. How have you dealt with them and how have they influenced or affected your life? Every aspect of life—physical, emotional, intellectual, behavioral, and spiritual—holds valuable, often irre-placeable, lessons for us.

Ideally, our task is to become introspective about the major transitions in our life, allowing the insights we've gained from them to remain with us. Being able to draw upon past events and experiences helps us to master the bigger picture.

- What are your life lessons?
- What lesson(s) had to be repeated many times before you acknowledged its existence? Did the lesson come as an "aha" moment, a revela-tory recognition, or after several attempts to do the same thing while hoping for a different outcome?

- When you finally got the lesson, how did that affect your thoughts, emotions, feelings, attitudes, behaviors, and beliefs?
- How have the messages of your life lessons inspired/encouraged/motivated you?
- How have your lessons changed the course of your life, your perspective of yourself, your view of the world?
- Have the life lessons you have learned taken you beyond your limitations?

RITES OF PASSAGE

*Opportunities to find deeper power within our-
selves come when life seems most challenging.*
Joseph Campbell

The classic *rite of passage* is a universal structuring
device existing within virtually every culture. Major life
events that honor changes in status or identity within
any given society are marked by the three-fold process
of separation, transition, and incorporation. We separate from the familiar, transition through unknown
territory, and return, transformed by the process.

Each rite of passage is, in essence, an initiation,
a death to rebirth drama. We die to something to be
born to something new. Mircea Eliade, historian of
religion and professor, noted that a series of such passage rites, or successive initiations, organizes an entire
life.

Years after Arnold van Gennep's *The Rites of Passage*
was published in 1908, anthropologist Victor Turner
focused his attention on the crucial middle stage of
transition, the "betwixt and between," as he referred

to it. Here, the real work of the passage, "to evoke creativity and change," takes place. As such, essentially, transition is the dynamic transformation of change.

Unfortunately, the loss of a vibrant culture of initiatory passage rites once inherent within virtually every known society has left many individuals these days without a prescribed roadmap for the "journey." Yet, many people have intuitively found their own way to create and perform personally meaningful rites of passage marking significant life transitions.

The *SHIFT* process expands the classic rite of passage, still an incredibly viable and valuable tool for navigating and finding safe passage through life's transitions:

- **S**eparating, we leave the familiar to enter into the unknown.
- **H**eeding the "call to adventure," we set out on a journey of self-discovery.
- **I**nviting opportunities and challenges, we "die" to our old selves.
- **F**inishing the task at hand, we return to our lives.
- **T**ransformed

It is essential to note that unlike the classic rite of passage or transition, which moves us from "here to there" in what appears to be linear fashion, *separation in the SHIFT process connotes movement in both directions. Before we can effectively move forward we must go backward, revisiting not only issues and events from the immediate past that may have influenced our thinking today, but more importantly, old programs from the distant past that have significantly altered the way we move through our life.*

Exercise: Creating a Rite of Passage

Rites of passage are powerful rituals for transition making. These universal structuring devices tell the individual and the society in which they live that a change has taken place. As previously noted, because these are largely *prescribed* initiation rites for major life cycle transitions (birth, coming of age, marriage, death, etc.) the changes involve moving from one identity and/or status to another.

A rite of passage may take the form of a creative ceremony specifically designed and performed to mark and honor a significant personal event or milestone. The ritual creativity employed may include the engagement of some or all of the senses, including rhythmic chanting, movement, and the use of symbols and imagery. Or, the rite of passage may spring forth of its own accord without formal ceremony, emerging from a deeply internal place, the subconscious, which ultimately colludes with the external world to find expression.

The symbolic enactment that is the hallmark of a rite of passage is deeply satisfying and empowering, restoring a sense of order and providing a feeling of safety, control, and connection to a higher spiritual source. What I want most to emphasize is the timeless quality of the rite of passage. Ordinary time and space are suspended, making room for the extraordinary to occur. We are literally, *present in the unknown.*

These are the stages of the classic rite of passage:

- **Setting the intention**: gaining clarity about the meaning and purpose of the transition
- **Separating from the familiar**: moving from the profane into the sacred, from the ordinary into the extraordinary
- **Crossing over the threshold**: stepping into unknown, uncharted territory; moving from the old toward the new
- **Reincorporating or reintegrating**: returning *transformed* to the everyday life

The creation and performance of a rite of passage take us out of the flow of our everyday routine world and invite us to rest, restore, and renew ourselves. Whether we choose to perform a rite of passage alone or in community with others, what is most important is that it is deeply felt and personally meaningful.

Ritual elements are specific universal tools used by many cultures for traditional ritual making (general categories are adapted from Cahill and Halpern). Choose one element, or combine several from this list, to create a desired simple ritual, such as lighting a candle, or an extremely complex rite of passage.

- **Purification:** cleansing with water, smudging, anointing with oil

- **Calling on Spirit:** prayer, seeking the blessings of ancestors
- **Calling in the Light:** lighting candles, a fire ceremony to consume the old
- **Sacrificing:** fasting, practicing silence, meditating
- **Gathering in Community**: giving or exchanging gifts, feasting
- **Worshipping**: praying, making offerings, creating altars
- **Communing**: singing, dancing, symbolic gestures to commune with Spirit
- **Exorcising**: getting rid of the negative by burning, burying, severing
- **Symbolically Dying**: crossing a threshold, moving in and out of a circle
- **Rebirth**: taking or receiving a new name, dressing in symbolic clothing

PART TWO: THE BASICS OF *SHIFT*

Understanding the basics of change provides the foundation for the **basics of *SHIFT*.** Since even the idea of change is often overwhelming and anxiety provoking, and for a few of us, something to be avoided at all cost, hopefully this overview has set your mind at ease about the prospect of change and the actual process of moving through it. Here are the main points to keep in mind.

- Change is inevitable and constantly happening. Change is the rule rather than the exception.
- Change is a cyclic process consisting of predictable stages. From beginning to end, this process returns to a point of origin, a new beginning, but one distinctly different from the one before it.
- As it refers to human development, this cyclic process is accompanied by predictable emotional states.
- According to Erickson's theory of psychosocial tasks/crises, even when an individual fails to complete a given task, carrying it unfinished into future steps, each subsequent stage provides added resources and opportunities to resolve old conflicts and crises.
- Transition is the process we make through change and is comprised of the three-stage process of separation, transition, and reintegration. The goal of transition is transformation.
- *SHIFT* is not a model or technique, but rather an expanded version of the transition process,

which allows for movement forward into the unknown, as well as backward, revisiting old issues and programs. It is a process based on the evolutionary unfolding of consciousness

The **basics of _SHIFT_** will further our understanding of the movement from change through transition and, ultimately, will help us effectively shift our focus as well as our consciousness in order to be transformed by the process. Our attention will be directed to:

- examining core beliefs about who we are and what our life should be like;
- understanding early programming;
- learning how to access and work with the subconscious;
- rewriting core beliefs in order to go beyond limiting beliefs;
- envisioning life as an organic, unfolding developmental process (rather than a linear progression of events) where not only do we move forward, but we also loop back in order to revisit and reframe past events and issues

UNDERSTANDING EARLY PROGRAMMING

> *The greatest revolution in our generation is the discovery that human beings, by changing the inner attitudes of their minds, can change the outer aspects of their lives.*
>
> **William James**

Recent research has shown that **you are what you believe.** This new way of looking at how we evolve as individuals is quite compelling theoretically. As a young psychiatrist, I was classically trained in traditional methods of psychotherapy. The often asked "emblematic" therapeutic question to the patient was, "How do you feel about that?" It didn't occur to me until many years into the process that feelings and emotions were actually different things, related but very different. Emotions are states of being, while feelings are our individual, very personal expressions of these emotions. Still it didn't occur to me to ask why feelings ran the gamut, from neutral to highly charged, from one person to the next.

What was it that determined someone's personal feelings? It took a question posed to me years later to identify what seemed to be missing. "Do patients talk about what they believe?" I realized that in most instances, they don't. In fact, most people are not sure what they really believe beyond that which they have been taught, that is, what they are *programmed* to believe.

What you perceive is what you believe. Your personal *perception* of reality is determined by the beliefs you hold. This does not necessarily make them real, except for the fact that you believe they are. Your beliefs create and dictate what your attitudes are. Your attitudes create and dictate how you respond—in other words, they dictate your feelings. Your feelings create and dictate how you behave.

Research has demonstrated that most emotional conditioning and habitual behaviors were set, in fact were *programmed,* very early in life by parents, peers, teachers, and the like. Basic core beliefs, behaviors, and attitudes held by these significant others are often simply accepted as "fact" and become the "truth." Children do not develop the capacity for critical *conscious* scrutiny until much later in life. Once "hardwired" within our subconscious mind, these beliefs, behaviors, and attitudes become firmly entrenched and the individual largely operates from the programs installed in early life. As adults, these old programs are still running our lives, even though they make no sense, limit our expectations, and may even be detrimental to our well-being.

In a child's brain the subconscious programs develop progressively—one skill building upon the necessary previous one. Astonishingly, a window of opportunity exists for each developmental program to be established. The window of opportunity for emotions is established very early in life—from birth to two years of age. The way we express our emotions—our feelings—may well reflect negative programming from way back when.

Trying to "talk" the subconscious into changing its mind may have some benefit, but often, traditional therapies leave something to be desired. We may gain some success through behaviorally bypassing these old programs and adapting new behaviors, but without accessing old programs, we never get to our core beliefs. Many of you who have been in therapy would probably say that your experience helped you gain insights, acquire tools, and develop skills to help you cope better. But many would also have to say that being in therapy, as well as reading self-help/improvement books, and attending seminars, while often interesting and inspirational, did not provide the long-term benefits that can only come from real change. And that means changing your core beliefs. Without that, it's simply on to the next therapy and on to the next self-help book.

Exercise: Opening to Your Core

Before you go digging for "buried treasure," take a few minutes to perform this exercise, which is designed to clear away unnecessary debris that may make your searching more difficult. This exercise will serve as a baseline measurement of where you are right now.

- Clarify what you believe/feel/think lies at the core of your being, in other words, who you really are. Do you know fully who you are? Do you take responsibility for bringing your own being into existence?
- If you're having trouble answering those questions, then continue. The recognition that you don't know is a very important awareness. Now focus your attention on this state of *not knowing*. Stay with this state of not knowing. What does it mean to you to *not know?*
- Ask your core being—whatever you consider your essential self to be—to express itself to you. Be open to whatever comes up. Your core being can express itself through the senses, for example, as a visual image, or through words that describe you, or symbols that represent who you are.
- Since the world as you know it is a creation of your beliefs, feelings, and thoughts, when you clear out a space, allowing yourself to open to the unknown, you release yourself from what you know/feel/believe already. When there is a field of "emptiness"—when you see open space rather than limiting barrier—new possibilities can emerge organically.

- When new possibilities come to you, try them on for size. Imagine yourself living these possibilities. Do they fit you better than the old ways? Now ask yourself again. Do you know fully who you are? Do you take responsibility for bringing your own being into existence?

Exercise: Archaeology—Returning to the Source

From your birth, you started on a journey. As a tiny being, you were pure, not yet aware of what was all around you. But eventually, your culture made its presence known, enveloping you in its language, customs, and beliefs. Over time, layer upon layer of your culture's artifacts surrounded the core of your authentic self. And eventually your individual awareness assumed the identity, the persona, of who you became. So who are you at the core of your being?

The "dig" allows archaeologists to remove layer upon layer of debris to discover significant artifacts that define a culture/society. Through this exercise, we are going on a "dig" to find the core "artifacts" of our own persona. After finding buried pieces of ourselves, we are then able to reincorporate these pieces back into our lives. Imagine yourself as you are today, at seventy or twenty, or anywhere in between. Describe yourself as you are now. Are you satisfied with who you are, or do you feel as if something is missing? If the latter, start digging. Although you will be using words to describe what you find, I want you to begin to "see" what you find in visual pictures, images, and symbols.

You will understand the importance of this way of seeing as we move along in the process.

- What are the "artifacts," the identifying traits that most clearly describe you through your life? Are these essentially the same throughout your life, or do the "artifacts" change from one period of your life to the next?
- Are there pieces of yourself that you neglected to pay attention to, didn't nurture? Are there parts of yourself that you discarded along the way? Were there life events that got in the way, preventing you from accomplishing what you wanted to do, or from adequately expressing a specific side of yourself?
- What specific activities, opportunities, or challenges were you not given a chance to do? What essential things do you feel you lacked? What do you feel you most needed but didn't get? What special skills or gifts were not acknowledged or encouraged?
- Describe five things you liked about yourself when you were a child. List five accomplishments of your childhood. Name three to five people that helped, encouraged, supported, or praised you.
- Describe five things you disliked most about yourself when you were a child. List five things you did that you wished had never happened. Name three to five people who demeaned you, made fun of you, discouraged you, or were mean to you.

Take your time with this exercise. Revisit this exercise often and regularly, especially as you gain new pieces of information and new insights about yourself along the way.

Note: Read through each of these exercises using your logical mind to just *think* about the answers. Later, you may want to meditate before you answer these questions, allowing your subconscious to find deeper meaning.

BRAINWAVES AND EARLY PROGRAMMING

The conflicts we generally experience in life are frequently related to our conscious efforts of trying to "force" changes upon our subconscious programming.

Bruce Lipton

How do we know where and how our beliefs began and how do we gain access to that place of origination? Brainwave theory sheds some light and provides some answers to these questions.

Brainwaves are measured by frequency, or speed (measured in cycles per second) and amplitude, or strength. They are categorized into four types: beta, alpha, theta, and delta. Beta brainwaves are the fastest and represent the kind of thinking and awareness we live in most of the time, the kind of activity absolutely necessary for our effective functioning in the outside world. Alpha brainwaves are slower and describe a state of relaxation and awareness, yet a detachment from active involvement. Theta brainwaves, slower yet, represent the subconscious mind, the seat of creativity and spiritual connection. And finally, delta brainwaves, slowest of all, are identified with the unconscious and deep sleep.

For the first two or so years of life, a child's brainwave functioning is largely in delta. Over the next several years, brainwaves progressively quicken. So between the ages of two and six, a child spends a lot of time in theta. Alpha activity is attained when the child develops an awareness of what is going on in the outside world. Finally, the abilities to analyze and function in the outside world correspond to the beta state and are achieved by adolescence. By adulthood, all of these are operative and are often seen in combination. According to researcher Anna Wise, even delta can combine with other brainwaves while we are awake and alert to produce a unique situation, which strives to comprehend, at the deepest unconscious level, that which cannot be understood through conscious thought processes.

The basics of a belief system are "programmed" during the first crucial years of life when a child lives most of the time in delta and theta. It is believed that the very slow delta state allows for the vast amount of information a child must learn and assimilate in the earliest years of life. Simply stated, very young children are sponges. Early programming of a child's subconscious prepares him/her to accept the beliefs of the culture into which he or she is born.

However, children at this tender age do not have the ability to analyze and challenge this information through conscious, critical thinking. And generally that's a good thing, given how much there is to learn. Conversely though, this inability to apply critical thinking to the information presented makes children readily accepting of whatever they hear, see, or are told. Consciousness is gradually achieved as development progresses and children mature, but by then, basic perceptions have already been deeply etched into the subconscious.

THE INNER LANGUAGE OF
THE SUBCONSCIOUS

Man's ultimate concern must be expressed symbolically because symbolic language alone is able to express the ultimate.
Paul Tillich

It is through symbols that man consciously or unconsciously lives, works and has his being.
Thomas Carlyle

The subconscious is recognized as the source of creativity, intuition, inspiration, inner knowing, interconnectedness, and spiritual enlightenment. Within this realm, reality shifts and expands, creating a matrix that is far more elastic and multi-dimensional than is perceived by the conscious mind. When we access and spend time within the subconscious, we are released from the confines of our logical, practical mind. The messages we receive from our dreams and the primordial symbols, or archetypes handed down to us from our ancestors, inform us about what is unique, authentic, and sacred to each of us. When we heed these messages, we are following the path of our soul's evolution.

These symbols and archetypes are essential elements of the *collective unconscious,* the universal intrapsychic structuring device innate to humans. It is as if the necessary acquired information learned by generations past is provided to us as a shortcut to our own evolution. Once something is learned in the evolution of human consciousness, it is not necessary to learned it again. It is inherent, forever after, with what it means to be human. The "eternal vocabulary" of the collective unconscious lives within us, always ready to offer hints and clues, suggestions and solutions. Learning to access the subconscious and to utilize its gifts fully can help us to "see" in a new way. Beyond our conscious mind and usual senses, the veil is lifted, revealing a world of unlimited possibilities.

What is so poignant here is that words are unnecessary to communicate or convey a message. The symbol, the representational picture or image, conveys the complete thought, concept, or ideal without the use of words to describe it; the proverbial, "a picture is worth a thousand words." This idea is tremendously powerful, for the way we "talk" to ourselves, our inner language, the way we know who we are, does not come from words, but rather from the timeless source within that *knows* who we are.

I've included this section on the subconscious for a good reason. First, a brief tutorial: The left hemisphere of the brain controls most of the neuromuscular and motor functioning of the right side. The right hemisphere controls the left side. But there is a huge difference as to the quality and character of each of the hemisphere's activity. The left hemisphere is largely involved with logical, analytic thinking, as in verbal and mathematical functions, while the right hemisphere is largely responsible for orientation in space, body image, recognition of faces, and artistic efforts.

The right side of the body, or *bodymind* as psychologist, original thinker, and author, Ken Dyctwald refers to it in his book of the same title, is identified with the masculine; traits associated with it are "assertiveness, aggressiveness and authoritarianism." The left side is considered feminine; traits associated with it are "emotionality, passivity, creative thought, and holistic expression."

A recent provocative theory proposes that a "*holistic, simultaneous, synthetic,* and *concrete* view of the world are the essential characteristics of a feminine outlook; *linear, sequential, reductionist,* and *abstract* thinking defines the masculine." Every person has the full capacity for both of these sets. Ideally, these should coexist equally, with neither more important nor dominant than the other. Leonard Shlain, the author of this theory, presents compelling evidence to suggest that the advent of the written word, and then the alphabet, shifted the mindset of cultures that were newly literate. *Word* and *image* are "complementary opposites"; that is, they are meant to coexist on equal footing. But while preliterate cultures exalted the Goddess and all things feminine, the shift toward the written word favored the masculine, and patriarchy ascended, and eventually dominated.

While this theory is rather impressive and may explain quite a lot about how things got to be the way they are, that's not my point. What is far more important to me is the idea that the subconscious (the right brain) utilizes symbolism and imagery to express itself and the devaluing of the image in favor of the word may have done more damage to the way we think as a collective humanity. This may explain the decline of *holistic expression* so identified with the right brain. It has been suggested that television, film, and the Internet may be reintroducing the images that account for a heightened awareness and expression of holism. We can only hope that's true.

The point of this is that I want you to begin "thinking" in a different way. I want you to become aware of the world of images and symbols, their meaning to you, and how their presence affects you. I want you to put the logical and practical aside for a while and to begin to imagine or envision without the use of words. For example, become aware of common symbols all around you, such as institutional logos, highway signs, religious images, and so on, and see how much you take them for granted. The *SHIFT* process utilizes imagery and symbols to help you access and **remember** subconscious material.

Exercise: Archetypal Themes

The word *archetype* literally means "first molded." Archetypes are original patterns from which things of the same kind that follow are modeled. There are impersonal (universal) archetypes, which relate to the whole of humanity, and personal archetypes, which are based on an individual's own unique experience. When humans resonate with certain archetypal themes, there is a strong emotional response, an awareness, or recognition of something that is familiar, and in the case of impersonal archetypes, ancient as well.

- What archetype(s) resonate with you?
- Why are you drawn to the archetype(s)? Can you identify the external influences that gave rise to your interest in the archetype(s)? For example, did they emerge from myths, fairy-tales, books, films, and so on?
- What characteristics are expressed by your favorite archetype(s) that represent who you are already?
- What characteristics of the archetype(s) are you drawn to and admire but are not expressed by you? Why? How can you incorporate more of what your archetype(s) expresses into your own personality?
- What characteristics of the archetype(s) represent your shadow side (referring to some of the unacceptable aspects of the objective psyche)? How do you express this part of yourself?
- If you could reconcile the polar opposites, the dual nature within the archetype(s), what would that mean?

Exercise: Tracking Your Dreams

We all dream, and when we do, we have an opportunity to access the creativity and intuition that lives within us. Many of us give far more credence to conscious waking life and undervalue the world of dreams; at times even dismissing them as far too fantastical or whimsical to be real. But if we think about it, the way we choose to see the world, both inner and outer, is a byproduct of our thoughts and perceptions, so it's nothing more or less than our own creation.

Dreams often bring important messages and provide valuable connection to something we would not have otherwise thought. Sometimes we have an inkling, some insight into what they mean; yet, other times, we have no real clue. The contents of our dreams often reveal meaningful clues, what is essential for us to know in order to work through to resolution the inner conflicts that cause or contribute to issues and problems that confront us in life. Recurring dreams, according to Jung, are manifestations of issues needing conscious attention in our waking life.

Many books advise keeping a dream journal, or paper and pen, next to your bed so when you awaken you can write your dreams down before you forget them. Beyond what we know and process in our waking life, our dreams give a first hand view of the workings of the subconscious. Go beyond recording dreams and the images they provide to research the dominant and/or recurrent themes and symbols that are personally meaningful to you. Take what you read about dream interpretation with a grain of salt, however; not everything will be applicable to or resonate with you. Remember, ultimately, it is how *you* interpret your dreams that matters.

REWRITING CORE BELIEFS

To transform reality, we must alter the one thing that is not fixed: the programs themselves. For our universe, these are what we call "beliefs." So in this way of thinking of things, belief becomes the software that programs reality."
Gregg Braden

The *subconscious mind* is a programmable "hard drive." The "programs" of our lives, which are largely stimulus-response behaviors, are downloaded into our subconscious. The subconscious does not rely on the outside world for its "knowing," so it can't differentiate between what is real and what is imagined. The subconscious remembers everything, is absolutely literal (which means there's no subtlety), and processes only in the *present tense*. It will look for and guide you to whatever you tell it. So you must be absolutely clear and specific in directing your subconscious to help you accomplish your goals. The subconscious mind uses imagination and feeling to communicate; *you can practice in your mind without ever doing the actions.*

Your *conscious mind,* on the other hand, is an evolutionary development of higher mammals. In humans, the conscious mind takes many years to develop and mature. It is logical and, as a thinking entity, uses words to communicate. It processes in the past, present, and future. The conscious mind directly perceives the outside world and takes in what it "sees." *The beliefs, attitudes, and behaviors that are programmed may override what our conscious mind desires. So to attain our conscious goals, the idea is to access the subconscious in order to go beyond our limitations—the limiting programs of the subconscious.*

The conscious mind experiences "reality" through the senses and, thus, its perception of what is possible is limited. Reprogramming old beliefs eliminates negative patterns. Although you still remember the negative event, the emotional response changes; the attachment you once had is essentially eliminated. When you change your belief, you change your response to life and what you believe you can achieve.

Exercise: Creative Visualization

This is a good example of how to use your imagination to help you create whatever you want to happen in your life. The technique has been around for a long time, has been well researched, and its usefulness has been demonstrated. For example, this is a popular technique in the preparation of seasoned athletes for competition.

Thought precedes creation; the idea guides energy in the physical world in order to create certain behaviors. There are three requirements for creative visualization to be fully effective: (1) the *desire* to create what you have decided to visualize, (2) the *belief* in what you have chosen to attain through your visualization and the certainty that you will attain it, and (3) the *acceptance* of having whatever you have visualized as your goal.

Anyone can utilize creative visualization to achieve a desired goal. Turn your attention to an area of your life upon which you want to focus. After moving into deep relaxation, examine this area just as it is in your present reality. What do you most want to change about it? What emotions and feelings would you want to accompany this change? List all the reasons that prevent you from creating/having this reality. Is it fear, anxiety, too much disruption to your life, to your relationships? Keep on going until you have identified all of the limiting reasons.

Now, imagine what you want to happen unfolding as you want it to be.

- Set your desired goal.
- Listen to your inner guidance to affirm that what you are asking for is what you really want, is positive, and is meant for your highest good.
- Create exactly what you want to happen *just as you want it to be.*
- Visualize this often and in as much detail as possible, utilizing all of your senses.
- Affirm what you create over and over again.

Remember, creative visualization is accomplished in the *first person* and in the *present tense*—it is happening to you now—so be extremely clear in the way you describe and visualize what you want to happen.

We all operate from our own individual point of view or perspective, a reality with which our mind feels comfortable. By realizing that we can consciously and actively alter our point of view through visualizing a desired outcome, we have an opportunity to shift perception in reality. Later, we will learn how to utilize meditation and guided imagery *to access subconscious material and bring it back to conscious awareness* in order to change our beliefs and go beyond our limitations.

WHAT DO YOU BELIEVE?

Men often become what they believe themselves to be. If I believe I cannot do something, it makes me incapable of doing it. But when I believe I can, then I acquire the ability to do it even if I didn't have it in the beginning.

Mahatma Gandhi

The Belief Inventory will help you clarify what you believe. You may feel that you already know this, but take the time to do the exercises and answer the series of questions. You may want to write your responses down so that you can refer to them later on. When you do this inventory for the first time, you are creating a baseline for yourself, in other words, where you are right now. Hopefully, some of your answers will be provocative enough for you to want to explore them in depth.

Whenever you are confronted by change, and transition is necessary to move forward, you may want to repeat the part(s) of the inventory that are relevant to the kind of change you are encountering. Remember, that what you believe is *not* written in stone and can be altered to better fit who you are within a specific stage or life circumstance.

1. The Self

- Create an inventory of who you believe yourself to be currently. Include within this inventory personal, historical, relational, spiritual, and intuitive aspects of yourself.
- Write a list of twenty things about yourself you know in your heart to be true. What determines the truth of these characteristics/traits to you? (Do you "just know," have you been repeatedly told these truths, or are they a result of self-examination and soul-searching?) Do you affirm these characteristics/traits in the way you live your life?
- Write a list of the things others believe to be true about you but you know are not accurate. Why have these characteristics/traits been reinforced? How do you effect a course correction with those things that you feel don't accurately fit you, or are core negative beliefs.

2. The Child

Returning to the "source" may help shed light on those special things that interested you and were meaningful to you when you were young.

- When you were a child, what did you love spending most of your time doing or being?

- What did you want to be when you grew up? What did you fantasize being/doing?
- What were you encouraged or discouraged from being or doing?
- Who was the person/people you admired the most? What did you admire the most about them?
- What "job/task" did you like doing the best/ the least?
- What do you wish you had been able to do but never got the chance?
- What were the things that you were especially recognized for?
- What were the things people neglected to recognize most about you?

3. **Intimate Relationships** are your mirrors. What you see reflected in significant others is often really more about you.
   - *The Present*—Focus on your current relationship, or the last one you had if you are not in a relationship at this time.
     o What does intimacy mean?
     o What are the qualities you value most about your partner?
     o What are the things you tolerate about your partner but don't really like?
     o What are the things you'd like to change most about your partner?
     o What are the things you'd like to change most about yourself in the relationship with your partner?

o What are things you wish your partner would do more?

o What are things you wish your partner would do less?

o What are you most concerned, worried, or anxious about in your relationship?

o What is your biggest fear about being in a relationship?

o What are the things you don't want your partner to know about you?

o What is the deepest, darkest secret that you never want to reveal, or be revealed?

o What are the things you'd want to change most about what you believe is required in order to have an intimate relationship?

- **The Past.** Repeat this exercise for any or all other significant relationships you've ever had. Is there a pattern that emerges? Are there any issues that specifically and consistently appear over and over again? If there are, take some time to reflect upon those issues and why they cause repeated concern.

- **The Future.** Project yourself into the relationship that you believe would best suit you. Imagine yourself in this relationship using all of your senses to make it feel as real as possible. How are you different than in past or present relationships? In this ideal relationship, what traits/characteristics would you choose your partner to possess?

4. Death and Dying

Having already created a loss timeline, let's focus now on your beliefs about death and dying. These are largely derived from our family of origin, religious community, and culture. Every culture has its own unique ideas and attitudes about death. Every religion has its own proscribed beliefs and behaviors, rituals and rites of passage, surrounding death.

Inevitably, what we learn early in life, as well as what we may actually experience, will have a direct effect upon what we believe and how we behave when we are confronted by death and dying. As with so many beliefs, we often don't stop to question their reality or validity. We just accept them as fact.

- When did you first become aware of death? What age were you?
- Was it the direct result of an event that occurred at a certain point in your life?
- Who or what had the greatest influence upon you around the issue of death and dying—family, religion, school, other?
- What attitude(s) did the family/religion/community impart to you about death?
- What belief(s) did the family/religion/community impart to you about death?
- Do you still adhere to these attitudes and beliefs from your early life?
- If not, what experience made you change the way you think and feel about death and dying?

- Moving forward in your life, what actual experiences have you had with death? How did those influence you?

- Have you had a personal experience with death such as a near death experience (NDE) or a brush with death as a result of illness or accident? If so, how were you changed by the experience?

- What is death? What does it mean to you?

5. Work/Career

Here are some reasons why people work: survival, money, power, the satisfaction of working in a team, being innovative/cutting edge, fulfilling a passion, rising in the ranks of a company, changing jobs every few years, being helpful to others/appreciated, making a difference in the world, being left alone, being your own boss. Where are you now? Are you now doing what you really want to be doing?

Answer these questions.

- What do you consider the most important aspect about working?

- What are the special traits/skills/gifts unique to you that your current work allows you to utilize/express?

- What are the traits/skills/gifts that your current job/work does not allow you to utilize or express?

- What job, career, or profession do you wish you had pursued?

- What got in the way of your pursuing/being what you thought about earlier in your life?
- If you had your choice to be/do anything at this point in your life what would that be?
- If you had your choice to pursue whatever career/profession/endeavor you wish, what would you have to do to accomplish that?

6. Creativity
- What is creativity?
- Do you consider yourself to be a creative person? If so, how do you express yourself?
- How did you express yourself creatively as a child? Did that expression find its way into your adult life? If not, why?
- What was your family's attitude about creativity and the creative process?
- Were you encouraged or discouraged in your creative expression/endeavors?
- Do you believe that there is some creative aspect of yourself that you have never pursued or expressed? If so, why haven't you?

7. Religion/Spirituality
- Do you consider yourself to be a religious person? What does this mean to you?
- Are you spiritual? If so, how does your spirituality express itself?
- Can you be both religious and spiritual?
- What did you learn from your family about religion and/or spirituality?

- How important is religion/spirituality to your life currently?
- What's positive about your religious/spiritual beliefs? What aspects of these are problematic for you?
- How have your religious/spiritual beliefs influenced the way you live your life?
- Can you understand and accept others' beliefs that are different from your own?

BELIEFS UNLIMITED

As long as you fight a symptom, it will become worse. If you take responsibility for what you are doing to yourself, how you produce your symptom, how you produce your illness, how you produce your existence—the very moment you get in touch with yourself—growth begins, integration begins.

Fritz Perls

John C. Lilly, M.D., was a physician, neurophysiologist, and pioneer of states of consciousness. A researcher with the National Institutes of Health and the Maryland Psychiatric Research Center, Lilly authored books on dolphin-human communication as well as on the exploration of the depths of our consciousness. It is not surprising to see the direction his life and work took considering the question that he had asked himself from the time he was a young man, "How can the mind render itself sufficiently objective to study itself?" Beyond his brilliant cutting-edge research and his "living on the edge" life, perhaps he is best known for his work *Programming and Metaprogramming the Human Biocomputer.* With all the recent references to the mind as a complex computer, it was Lilly, in fact, who coined the word *biocomputer.*

Very simplistically, to Lilly's way of thinking, all humans who reach adulthood are programmed biocomputers. However, we all have the capacity to "self-program" the biocomputer and, therefore, create new programs and revise old programs. This exercise, created by Lilly will begin to help you go beyond your beliefs and the structure that holds them in place. As stated before, our reality is a creation of our beliefs, feelings, and thoughts. When we allow our self to open to the unknown, we release our self from what we already think, feel, and believe. When there is a field of "emptiness," where we are able to see space rather than a barrier, new possibilities can emerge; we are free to go beyond our limiting beliefs.

(Prerecord this exercise.) Lilly suggested recording this five consecutive times and listening to it, often and regularly:

> *In the province of the mind, what one believes to be true either is true or becomes true within certain limits, to be found experientially and experimentally. These limits are beliefs to be transcended.*
>
> *Hidden from one's self is a covert set of beliefs that control one's thinking, one's actions, and one's feelings. The covert set of hidden beliefs is the limiting set of beliefs to be transcended. To transcend one's limiting set, one establishes an open-ended set of beliefs about the unknown.*

The unknown exists in one's goals for changing one's self, in the means for changing, in the use of others for the change, in one's capacity to change, in one's orientation toward change, in one's elimination of hindrances to change, in one's assimilation of the aids to change, in one's use of the impulse to change, in one's need for changing, in the possibilities of change, in the form of change itself, and in the substance of change and of changing.

The unknown exists in one's goals for changing one's self, in the means for that change, in the use of others in the changing, in one's capacity for changing one's self, in one's orientation toward changes, in the elimination of hindrances to changing, in one's assimilation of the aids to changing, in one's impulses toward changing one's self and undergoing changes, in one's needs for change, in the possibilities for change, in the form of the changes themselves, and in the substance of the changes and of changing itself.

There are unknowns in my goals toward changing. There are unknowns in my means of changing. There are unknowns in my relations with others in changing. There are unknowns in my capacity for changing. There are unknowns in my orientation toward changing. There are unknowns in my assimilation of changes. There are unknowns in my needs for changing. There are unknowns in the possibilities of me changing. There are unknowns in the forms into which changing will put me. There are unknowns in the substance of the changes that I will undergo, in my substance after changes.

My disbelief in all these unknowns is a limiting belief, preventing my transcending my limits. My disbelief in these unknowns is a belief, a limiting belief, preventing my transcending my limits.

By allowing there are no limits; no limits to thinking, no limits to feeling, no limits to movement. By allowing, there are no limits. There are no limits to thinking, no limits to feeling, no limits to movement.

That which is not allowed is forbidden. That which is allowed, exists. In allowing no limits, there are no limits. That which is forbidden is not allowed. That which is not allowed is forbidden. That which exists is allowed. That which is allowed, exists. In allowing no limits, there are no limits. That which is not allowed is forbidden. That which is forbidden is not allowed. That which is allowed, exists. That which exists is allowed. To allow no limits, there are no limits. No limits allowed. No limits exist.

In the province of the mind, what one believes to be true either is true or becomes true. In the province of the mind, there are no limits. In the province of the mind, what one believes to be true is true or becomes true. There are no limits. *

Pay particular attention to the idea of a "covert set of beliefs." This is the program that determines our thinking, feelings, and action. And let's face it, we're taught that the unknown is a place to be feared. That's a belief many of us seem to have acquired. However, when we establish the possibility of "unknowns" we're effectively opening ourselves up to transcend whatever limiting beliefs we hold.

The notions of what is *allowed exists* and what is *not allowed* is *forbidden* are tremendously powerful.

Forbidden implies taboo. We are concerned here with beliefs that are imposed and that leave no room for an alternative perspective or point of view. Think about all of the things you were overtly or covertly instructed to avoid; how much of your behavior was modified, or even extinguished. (Of course, *some* conditioning is necessary for the purposes of survival and socialization.) The messaging could run as deep as an absolute prohibition carrying severe punishment, real or imagined, if not obeyed, to a milder form, such as disapproval or pressure to comply and conform, which, nonetheless, is very limiting.

After you have passively listened to this exercise several times, you may want to actively work with the elements contained within it. This exercise actively takes these various elements, referred to as "mentations" by Lilly, and utilizes them to create a structure, consisting of a series of ordered questions meant to challenge held beliefs, and to effectively change them. Think of this exercise as a way to "self dialogue." Ask yourself the questions and answer the questions, much as you would do with a therapist.

Choose any issue/behavior you want to address. Ask these questions in the order in which they appear in the Beliefs Unlimited exercise.

- What are my *goals* when I engage in this behavior/way of thinking, feeling, believing, or acting? In other words, what do I get out of doing it?
- What are the *means* to stop this behavior? What do I need to do to stop?

- What is my *charisma* (meaning my relationship with other people and the way I utilize that relationship) that allows me to continue this behavior, or to stop this behavior?

- Do I have the *capacity* to stop this behavior? How do I know I can stop?

- What is my *orientation*, when I engage in this behavior, or when I stop this behavior? Where is this behavior leading me in each case?

- What do I have to *eliminate* to stop this behavior? What behavior(s) do I need to let go in order to stop doing what I'm doing?

- What do I have to *assimilate* to stop this behavior? What must I absorb/adopt to change this conditioned behavior?

- What must I do to bring my *impulses* in line with stopping this behavior? How do I extinguish the impulses/desire that perpetuates the behavior?

- What are my *needs* when I engage in this behavior and when I stop this behavior? What habitual activities that support this behavior must be eliminated?

- What are the other *possibilities* in relationship to this behavior? What positive behaviors can potentially replace old negative patterns of behavior?

- What is the *form* this behavior takes? Describe detail-by-detail how this behavior is carried out on an ongoing basis. Is this behavior really important to your being?

- What is the *substance* of this behavior? What does this negative, potentially dangerous behavior really have to do with who I am?

Lilly addressed inner realities by constructing a model that included the old reality as well as the new one. In essence, this critical, but honest questioning of one's motivation and behavior creates a new program, one that exposes the negative side of the behavior that's always been there.

* By permission; John C. Lilly, *The Center of the Cyclone*, Berkeley, CA: Ronin Publishing, 1972: 128-129.

PART THREE: THE *SHIFT* PROCESS

Before beginning any process, it's a good idea to envision that process within a broader context. The first part of this book provided general information to help you place the idea of change within a bigger picture, universally recognized and understood. There is nothing like the continuity and reliability of ancient wisdom to assure us that we are on the right track, that we are living a universal model of what it is to be human.

The second part of the book focused attention on new ways of looking at how we got to be the way we are, and how we can change that. Beyond what we already know about human psychosocial/psycho-spiritual development, the theories that describe and explain why we are the way we are, research and technology over the last half century has expanded both our theoretical understanding of how we develop and grow, but more importantly, has encouraged a more active participation, a movement personally and collectively, toward a higher consciousness.

In addition to the exercises you have already done, this last part of the book provides a few essential tools to help you structure your own process as you move from transition to transition. Although each of you will have your own unique experience of this process, the archetype of the journey will be the same.

THE ROADMAP

The good life is a process, not a state of being.
It is a direction, not a destination.
Carl Rogers

You wouldn't think about starting out on a trip without having some idea where you're going and how to get there. There are specific directions you have to follow. These days, with detailed maps and GPS helping us navigate, that's made all too easy. Of course, if you really don't care where you're going, maybe it doesn't really matter where you end up. And in that case, you can just get into your car, point it in any direction, and hope for the best. Who knows...you might just luck out.

I think you're getting my point. Your life is a journey with lots of stops along the way and if you could have some idea what to expect, at least some of the time, you might feel a lot better about the whole thing. The image of the journey is so much a part of our language that I don't think we even stop to think anymore about what we're actually saying. There are crossroads, back roads, peak experiences, mountains to climb, valleys of despair, deserts and oases, wildernesses and waste-lands, rivers to cross, forks in the road, detours, dead ends, and the open road. They're all descriptive of places we've been. Wouldn't it be nice to know before-hand what lies ahead in order to avoid an unpleasant, or difficult, or seemingly insurmountable, obstacle on our path?

I find it nothing short of amazing that before we buy a car, a computer, or any other sort-after device, we consult with experts, friends, and consumer reports to get all the information we will need to make an informed decision. This is not so when it comes to taking responsibility for ourselves and making healthy decisions for our own well-being and happiness.

What's also amazing is that several years of our early education is spent learning multiplication tables and long division when, at the very least, some of that time could be spent learning necessary life skills, such as how to be a responsible person—not only for our own good, but for that of society as well—or effective decision-making. Many adults still find it hard to make basic and essential decisions for their life.

Let me suggest that we need to find the means to teach the lessons by reframing history or mythol-ogy, or any subject for that matter, in such a way that the stories that are told carry a deeper message. It's not about learning the details and the facts but about understanding the underlying meaning.

For example, *The Odyssey* is not just about the trav-els and adventures of the Greek hero, Odysseus. It is a story about life unfolding, about transitions. It's a great example of one huge rite of passage, or if you choose, several consecutive passage rites that encompass all of the adventures and tasks of the journey for the hero. But in actuality, the events are as dependent, if not more so, on the choices made by the people left behind, namely the women and the common folk, as on the actions of the heroes. Interestingly, the original poem was composed in the oral tradition and was originally sung by a poet/singer more than read.

So far, whenever applicable, I have asked you to try to envision things, not in words but in images. Earlier, you created a Life Timeline to describe the major transitions in your life. This was probably a graph or chart with words or descriptions to help you categorize and define your experience. Now I want you to create a Road Map that shows the course of your life thus far. On a blank piece of paper, create a map of your life, complete with physical landmarks, to depict places you've been. Include mountains, valleys, rivers, deserts, back roads, and detours. Make sure the paper is large enough to allow you to spread out. Notice directions and change of directions. How many of the directional changes did you initiate and how many directional changes and course corrections were imposed upon you? Notice how often you returned to the same old places. Did you return due to habit or necessity? Were difficult passages overcome?

Your personal road map depicts your journey so far. It shows you where you've been and where you've come from to arrive at this moment. **YOU ARE HERE**.

The road map for the next leg of your journey starts **HERE**. Understanding the nature of change from a universal perspective, rather than from the narrower perspective of our own private experience, helps create a sense of familiarity and predictability. No more shock or surprise or chaos when change comes; you now have some idea about what to expect and what to do. Having an understanding about *how we learn* also helps to frame our thinking about why and how we believe and behave the way we do in a completely new way, one that affords us a far better command of what we do with what happens to us. The *SHIFT* process will provide a reliable structure for you to process change and successfully accomplish transition.

BEING PRESENT

Understanding comes into being from the now,
the present, which is always timeless.
Krishnamurti

The present is *this* exact moment. It does not consider what just happened or what will happen in the
next moment. It is the pause between life happening; it is the now. The present goes beyond words and
actions. It is *you* communicating with *you.* All of the
external accoutrements of being human are about
relating to the world around you—to people, to places,
to things. Being present to yourself means *being* in conscious moment awareness. Learning to *be present* is the
foundation of who you are in this life unfolding.

In mythology, the Roman god Janus (from Ianus,
meaning archway) presided over gates, doors, bridges,
as well as endings and beginnings. Depicted with two
heads facing in opposite directions, legend has it that
Janus was gifted with the ability to see the past as well
as the future. Symbolically, Janus represents change
and transition.

January, the New Year, is always a good time—a built-in annual reminder—to sit with yourself and reflect on the past year, or just the past in general. How did this last year stack up compared to others? Did you actually do what you resolved to do just one short year ago? Have you resolved the big issues of your past in order for you to move forward? Most of us are quick to make resolutions that we all too often don't keep. And we keep on doing that year after year, very often with the same resolutions. You don't have to wait for each January to roll around to stop and reflect on where you are in your life. You can do that anytime.

Sitting with yourself is not as easy as it sounds. In fact, it's often very hard to do since most of life as we know it is organized in a "here and there" fashion. We are forever coming and going—coming from somewhere to go somewhere. In reality, though, there is a *stillpoint* between the past and the future—and that is the present. It's important to set aside the time to just *be*, although for many of us that's a difficult task since we're so unpracticed at doing it. And frankly, even the thought of it makes us anxious.

But it's only in that place that we can ask ourselves what we really want to happen...and get an answer. That answer comes from our own "still, small voice" that is the source of our inner knowing. That source is the place of no opinion, no reaction, no judgment or prejudice. When the answer comes we can begin to make plans, to set our course, for the meaningful changes we want to occur and for the things we wish to accomplish.

Meditation: The Practice of Presence

Meditation has long been utilized as a means to quiet the mind and get in touch with ourselves on a deep level. It is a proven practice that helps us (1) learn to be present and (2) access the subconscious mind. Without the stimulation of the external world constantly pulling at us, we have the opportunity just to be present with ourselves, allowing access to our own intuitive, creative, and spiritual awareness. There is nothing new about what meditation is and/or about the myriad benefits it provides. But it's probably safe to say that most of us don't know what happens during meditation, why it works, or how we can consciously tap into our inner stores of wisdom at will.

Some thirty-five years ago, Herbert Benson, M.D., sought a solution to the plague of medical complications caused by stress. The blending of sound scientific data and ancient teachings from both Eastern and Western traditions resulted in *The Relaxation Response.* This physiologic response is innate within all humans and can be evoked through several different techniques. Measuring such factors as oxygen consumption, heart rate, respiratory rate, blood pressure, and alpha brain waves leave no doubt as to the efficacy and beneficial effects of relaxation on the human organism.

While there are many ways to practice meditation, the method provided by *The Relaxation Response* is appealing since it is simple and practical for anyone, anytime. The elements required are *a quiet environment, a mental device, a passive attitude,* and *a comfortable position.* To perform your practice, sit comfortably with eyes closed. Relax your muscles, breathe through your nose, say the word "ONE" after each in-out breath, and sit passively for ten to twenty minutes, once or twice a day. That's it.

Of course, there are any number of ways to practice. Having a mantra to recite, or just observing your breath without saying anything are techniques used by many. For those of you who have an aversion to sitting still or just feel like you are incapable of doing it, perhaps walking meditation may work for you. It's a bit harder because you are moving and may be easily distracted by what you observe around you. But if you can stay focused on just what is there before you, not how you think about or describe what you see or sense, this method may work for you. In fact, for some spiritual teachers, meditation is practicing mindfulness about *whatever* it is you are doing in any given moment.

I feel compelled to comment on the concepts of being present and on the practice of meditation. There's nothing new about what I'm saying here. Hundreds of people have written on these topics, so much so that it feels strange to be doing the same without hoping for a different outcome for you after you've read about them this time. What I'm saying is that I suspect that although many of you may have taken the concept of presence and the practice of meditation to heart, I also know that many of you will read the words and agree with the basic ideas but will not allow yourself the time or opportunity to participate in doing either or both. I believe it's worth a try, since if you can't be present for yourself, how will you know what *you* really want, and how will you know how to make that happen for yourself? Your life springs forth from you and only you, definitely not from someone or something outside of yourself.

WHO LOOKS INSIDE, AWAKES

Carl Jung

Beyond the practice of meditation to attain present moment awareness, there is a form of meditation that uses guided imagery to achieve a state of relaxation, as well as to gain access to the subconscious. Anna Wise is a pioneer in the field of brain wave research and worked closely with her mentor, C. Maxwell Cade from 1973 to 1981 as he gathered research and developed the Awakened Mind. Cade was a psychobiologist, biophysicist, and the progenitor of British EEG biofeedback in the 1970s. Wise eventually returned to the United States to develop her own work based on the Awakened Mind model.

Cade measured the brain wave patterns of spiritual teachers, healers, practiced meditators and hundreds of his own students. According to Wise, he identified a pattern that seemed to go beyond meditation, demonstrating the "lucid awareness" of meditation "coexistent with thought processes." Beta is the "thinking" mind while alpha, theta, and delta in combination, is the "meditating" mind. So those healers and teachers that Cade studied were thinking and meditating at the same time while maintaining an open flow of communication between the two. Now this is big stuff since most of us have trouble remembering in beta, our thinking state, what happened in theta, our subconscious state. Just try to remember a dream a while after you've woken up, or a repressed memory.

Wise went on to expand the work and study creative artists, scientists, and high-level corporate executives, and concluded that the "brain wave patterns of high performance, of creativity, the bursts of peak experience" were the one and the same that the previously researched masters actually lived in most of the time.

While I certainly believe that mastering brain waves is a great tool for creating a mind set that helps you perform optimally, the main point for us to take away is that we are capable of *learning* how to train the mind to utilize brain wave patterns in order to create the "state and content of consciousness" that we want, when we want it. Think about our discussion of early programming. Here is a tool you can use to gain access to subconscious material (and early programs) and bring them back to consciousness where you can then work with them.

To be fair, there are many brain entrainment programs available. I recommend this work because of its sound basis in research, Cade's early involvement in biofeedback, the use of meditation in the form of guided meditation or creative visualization (which many of you are familiar with already) because it asks for your responsible involvement as you learn, and because I've experienced working with the technique and Anna Wise herself.

Wise's work demonstrates how *alpha* brainwaves serve as the bridge from the conscious mind to the subconscious (theta); the movement from alpha to theta allows the uncovering of material hidden from conscious view. When we meditate with guided imagery, we essentially leave the conscious world (beta) behind, and achieve alpha by allowing ourselves to enter into deep relaxation. Achieving alpha is enhanced through "sensualization," using all of the senses in a creative visualization. Deepening theta, Wise advises using imagery that takes you *down, around, under, over, up, into,* and *through.*

The following meditation is meant to help center you anytime, specifically as a tool to use before doing any of the exercises in this book, to physically and emotionally ground you. Beyond what you have ever understood about meditation, the imagery within it is designed to help quiet your mind and access your inner wisdom by reaching down into the deepest recesses of your mind.

The Bridge Meditation

Prerecord this meditation, or have someone read it to you.

Make sure that nothing can disturb you during your meditation. Sit comfortably in a chair, feet flat on the floor, hands resting next to you, or on your knees. If you meditate regularly, position yourself as you usually do. Close your eyes. Closed-eyed meditation allows you to shut out external stimuli in order to more readily go within.

Scan your body from your feet to your head for any tension you might be holding. If there is stress anywhere, ask that part of your body to let go of its tension.

Now, direct your attention to your breath. Take a deep breath and let it course through you. Release any tension as you exhale. Do this again. Breathe in... breathe out. Breathe in...breathe out, once again.

Allow your thoughts and feelings to fade away.

Now picture yourself as you were just a few moments ago, just before you started this meditation. Think about what you were doing—your actions, interactions, and conversations with others. Really think about this fully, using all of your senses. So often we are operating on automatic pilot without giving any real thought to what we're doing, why we're doing it, and what the significance is of the thoughts, actions, and feelings that we're experiencing. So much of our time is spent this way. Take your time. Really let yourself have this experience. Now, let it go.

For a while, you will hear protests—voices in your head, lists of things to do, bits and pieces of your life, trying to get your attention. Gently tell these intrusions to stop. Keep on reminding them about this until the voices get quieter and finally recede into the background. Now, literally, turn yourself away from them. Leave them behind you. You are going on a journey.

You find yourself in a lush garden overlooking a vast magnificent ocean. Look around you and allow yourself to absorb the sheer perfection of nature. The air is warm and wonderfully scented—the fragrance of flowers. Take a deep breath. Allow yourself to be filled with the sweetness of the scent. As the salty breeze gently blows, feel the balmy air caress your skin. Taste the ocean. Listen to the sounds of the world around you.

When you are ready, turn your attention to the set of steps that will take you down to another stunning garden. Rest here a while, allowing all of your senses to soak in the beauty and peace. Allow yourself to experience this place fully. Notice the colors, the sounds, and scents all around you.

One last time, turn your attention to another set of steps. At the bottom, you find yourself in a thick, dark wood. Before you is a bridge, a simple footbridge over a gently flowing body of water. Turn your attention to the bridge. You must cross it to find what you are looking for. You're not sure what that is, but that doesn't matter.

The air feels cooler, fresher, and is pleasantly scented. The sound of the bubbling waters calms and relaxes you. Begin to walk, one foot after the other. You focus on the sound—one foot, then the other, as they contact the uneven wooden slats you walk upon. You walk, trusting you will find your way. The bridge stretches on before you. As you move forward, you are aware of your surroundings, but cannot see where the bridge ends, or what lies beyond it. In fact, the place where you are going is shrouded in fog and mist.

You continue until the bridge is behind you. Suddenly, the fog lifts and a vast panorama opens before you. Take in the beauty and mystery of this place, using all of your senses. Everything you can imagine exists here. It is only for you to find what you are looking for. Take your time exploring this immensely rich, fertile place. Where you go and how you choose to use your time here is totally up to you.

You may wish to explore without agenda or purpose, just simply taking in everything that comes your way. Or, you may be looking for answers to something you may have wondered about for a very long time. If this is so, allow yourself as much time as you need to find where you're meant to be. And go there. Notice whatever comes up for you—the impressions, images, and sounds that emerge. You may not remember them, so now find a symbol that reminds you, a symbol that embodies this experience, and remember that to take back with you.

This is the place of spirit, the seat of your soul. This is the place of your creative self. This is the place of your inner knowing and the repository of all wisdom. This is the place where your pure self resides. This is the place of interconnection and harmony with all. Remember your experiences here. And know that you are always welcome here.

When you are ready, look around one more time, taking away with you a heightened awareness of *what is*. Remember this. Retrace your steps and find the bridge. Begin your journey back. Slowly allow yourself to reenter the everyday world in which you live.

Remember the protesters. They are waiting to get your attention. But before you let them back in, make sure to ground your experience in this meditation by writing, drawing, or talking about it. Key words, images, and symbols will help you consciously remember what has happened so that it does not slip back into your subconscious.

Note: For those of you in some form of "talk" therapy, I would suggest taking the time before your therapy session to do some kind of relaxation/meditation exercise. Some therapists even begin sessions this way. Too often, people arrive at a therapy session in a "beta" state of mind, meaning they are still preoccupied with the analytical thinking necessary for engaging the tasks of everyday life. But to optimize the work of therapy, dipping into the vast subconscious for information and insight, it's a good idea to quiet the mind, slowing the brainwave activity down to more easily access this realm.

THE SHAPE OF *SHIFT*

> *Living is the constant adjustment of thought to life and life to thought in such a way that we are always growing, always experiencing new things in the old and old things in the new. Thus life is always new.*
>
> **Thomas Merton**

Our lives are shaped by symbols, which are the primordial images that have been inherited from our ancestors and are deeply ingrained within the collective unconscious. When we trace the use of symbols from ancient times to the present, it becomes clear that it is the spiral, perhaps even more specifically than the circle, that defines the form and force of life in everything, including the development of consciousness. In *The Mystic Spiral,* Jill Purce remarks, "The spiral tendency within each one of us is the longing for and growth toward wholeness. Every whole is cyclic, and has a beginning, a middle, and end. It starts from a point, expands and differentiates, contracts and disappears into the point once more. Such a pattern is that of our lifetime and may well be that of our universe."

The spiral *movement* is responsible for the creation of many forms in nature, including the solar systems, along with their suns and planets, the galaxies, and the vortical flow of water. Cycles and movements within the macrocosm provide the model for the cyclic nature of the microcosmic individual life. For Purce, within the spiral *form* "the potential for movement in either direction manifests as choice"—the spiral upward or the vortex downward, as well as the directional right or left along the vertical axis. The spiral *process* represents the course of evolution, humanity's developmental climb to realize heightened consciousness.

The spiral *tendency* exists within each of us, and is exhibited within the evolution of our own consciousness. If we imagine our individual life along a continuum through time, we can envision a straight line. But in reality, the cyclic nature of life allows for a return, as well as a continuous movement forward; and so we can effectively move in two directions. Since any transition moves us through successive stages to completion, we can assume that transformation sees the individual returned to his/her life, but in a state vastly different from how they were before the transition. The spiral movement, thus, describes not only the movement forward, but also a return to a *higher* level, another successive winding upward.

Using the same principles, we can move in the opposite direction as well. Remember the spiral movement can take us up or down, left or right. We can start at a point of origin along the continuum and travel backward to clarify issues, find answers, and gain insights from the past that will help us moving forward. Or, we can utilize what we've already learned in order to revisit unfinished business and unresolved issues, and hopefully, apply this new information to help shift our perspective. Although it is our goal to grow, to spiral upward, at times we regress, spiraling downward. Neither one is a permanent state; a point of origin, where we had once been, is always within our view and capacity. The potential for and the capacity to change is always available to us.

In attempting to understand the evolution of consciousness for humanity as a whole, philosopher, author, and visionary Ken Wilber's extensive body of research and writings tap into and expand the theoretical work of several cutting edge researchers. Wilber's integral theory of consciousness pushes beyond linear thinking to embrace *Spiral Dynamics*. In *A Theory of Everything*, borrowing from the work of Beck and Cowan (which builds on the work of Clare Graves), he describes human development as a movement through eight general stages, called *memes*, which are "not rigid levels but flowing waves, with much overlap and interweaving, resulting in a meshwork or dynamic spiral of consciousness unfolding." For Wilber, the natural tendency of each wave is to "transcend and include." Each wave transcends the one that preceded it, yet includes all of those previous capacities and strategies, and the potential of each of these stages is available to everyone.

The shape of *SHIFT* for the individual mirrors the shape of human consciousness unfolding. The capacity and potential of everything we have ever known, have ever experienced, or have ever been remains within us. We can always spiral around to find the answer or the solution.

The "mystic spiral" describes the development of humanity's psycho-spiritual unfolding as well. It is no mistake that as we strive to recapture a sacred balance between the rational and the intuitive, symbols reemerge to help us accomplish this. The labyrinth is an ancient meditative tool to describe many things: the cosmos, the Mother, the Way—the journey through life. This archetypal tool has resurfaced from our collective unconscious to find ever-increasing expression everywhere. What is so compelling about the labyrinth is that it fully embodies the archetype by engaging both subconscious and conscious. The labyrinth creates a physical space, a container that allows access to the subconscious through conscious intention, through the physical act of "walking the archetype."

Moving outward to ever increasing expanses, we go further and further to the edge; the movement inward integrates what we have assimilated from our outward journey and from our successive windings. Constant to this process, like the axis our planet revolves upon, is the center, a homecoming to the self.

THE PROCESS

You have to leave home to find home.

Our journeys are both inner and outer. The events of the outer journey, the cumulative transitions of a lifetime, will be somewhat similar for all of us who share the human experience. Our inner journey is a much more private affair. The road map is a reliable context within which to place and measure your own experiences. The *SHIFT* process is your traveling companion. Whether you travel far from home to find what you're looking for, or stay right where you are, traveling deeply into the farthest recesses of your mind, the process will be with you to offer guidance and assistance.

Here are some key points to keep in mind even before you begin the process:

- In your decision to undertake the journey, you've sown the seeds of your transformation.
- Getting the "call" can come from both external and internal events. Often the changes in your

life come from your basic need requirements; you may need to change where you live, your job, and/or your life circumstances to ensure your continued survival. Those basic changes will inevitably necessitate many other changes in order to completely carry you into your new situation. On the other hand, the "call" may be your inner voice telling you it's time to move again, meaning that you are ready to ascend to a level higher than the one in which you're currently situated.

- Transition can be a vehicle, a conscious catalyst to set a desired goal in motion. For example, you may have been held back from making changes in your life for any number of reasons—too disruptive to your life, non-negotiable with significant others, or restrictive financial considerations. But when change is thrust upon you and your life is turned upside-down, or the life you once knew is gone, there may be a window of opportunity to start over again, this time attending to what you really want out of life.

- Fear of the unknown is totally rational. Otherwise, we would be rushing into places we should not go. Rational fear allows us to cautiously explore what we have little or no idea about so that we can make careful and sound decisions about how to best proceed.

- The preparation for the journey requires that you take only what you absolutely need with you. In part, this means assessing the situation to understand your options fully *before* you actually make the transition. When you process in this way, you streamline your efforts so that you can fully focus your attention on the task at hand. Otherwise, you will be wasting a lot of time and energy trying to figure things out instead of maintaining total clarity for the work of the transition, which is living in the unknown. You want to keep yourself open for the opportunities.

- Beyond any spiritual connotation, *enlightenment* means to achieve clarity, to shed light on that which had been unknown. Travelling "light" means leaving your excess baggage behind, before you start your journey. Take only the bare essentials.

- Gain reasonable closure on what is left behind. Although you may experience any number of emotions around this, try to understand the reason and purpose for the existence of this experience in your life. Try to see its value to you, although you might have previously thought of it as nothing more than an obstacle in your path, or as an albatross around your neck.

- Your missteps and mistakes, your disappointments and disasters, are the raw material for new opportunities and challenges.

- *Transformation* literally means to move across or through in order to change the shape. With the transition completed, the idea is to bring a new order, to create a new shape to your life.

Reviewing the Process

This review is for the *first time* you read the material and do the exercises. What is covered should be thought of as a broad overview of many aspects of your life. Doing the exercises serves as a baseline for future use. For any subsequent time you review this material, for example, anticipating another transition, you can tailor the process to meet your specific needs.

1. Before you embark on your next transition, map your trip as best you can, knowing that things don't always work out as you plan or hope they will. Have a realistic expectation and reasonable timetable for the change to occur through transition. Some transitions take a relatively short period of time; others take years, sometimes decades, and in rare cases, a lifetime.

2. Take the time to *review* what you've learned about **change** and your response to it to make the best possible choices and decisions, unless, of course, the change is one that places you in imminent danger, such as life-threatening illness, unexpected personal crisis, or natural disasters, where you have no choice but to take immediate action. In that case, once the necessary actions are taken and the dust finally settles, you can then go back and review in order

to figure out what the transition meant and what to do next.

3. Create a **Life Timeline** reflecting major life transitions, and a **Loss Timeline** reflecting loss as the main theme of the transition. Pay special attention to the main emotions for each of these transitions and how you expressed them through your feelings.

4. Define your **Life Themes** and **Life Lessons.** This goes well beyond charting the chronological order, the "facts" of your life. Themes are easily recognizable, especially when they present as recurring and repetitive behaviors. Doing the same thing over and over again will not bring a different result. Again, you may get lucky. What have you learned from life so far and how does that impact your life moving forward?

5. Emotions and feelings are commonly thought to be the most reliable indicators of who you are and how you express yourself. Belief systems theory asks you to go a step beyond this to identify what you believe, or rather what you were *programmed* to believe. The material presented about beliefs may or may not change how you feel about what you believe, but at the very least, spending the time to question yourself about this is important at this point. Often the actions we take and the choices and decisions we make are based on ideas that no longer serve us, if they ever did in the first place. Going beyond limiting beliefs may pave the way

for changing the way you transition moving forward. **Opening to Your Core** will help you understand what you know, but more importantly, what you don't know. Learning to deal with the unknown is an essential skill in successful transition-making. **Archaeology: Returning to the Source** will help you begin finding missing pieces of yourself.

6. **The Belief Inventory** will give you a brief overview of what you believe about several key areas in your life. You can expand upon these to create your own inventory for the specific area that is reflected within a major transition you are going through.

7. **The Beliefs Unlimited** meditation and exercise will help you reframe behaviors in a step-by-step, straightforward new way that will challenge how you've been programmed, or have programmed yourself.

8. Since the archetype for life is the journey, **The Road Map** will help you plan your life moving forward much as you would prepare for a trip. Charting your trip tells you where you've been so far, where you're intending to go, what your obstacles have been, and places you keep returning to on your journey. Drawing your journey, or using guided imagery or creative visualization, allows you to visually see or imagine where you've been, and then envision where you want to go.

9. Meditation is key in learning present moment awareness. **Being Present** firmly roots you in the here and now, encouraging you to move through your life mindfully. Accessing the subconscious provides rich raw material that will help you go beyond limiting beliefs.

10. **Spiral Movement** describes much of the natural flow of the universe and is the shape of the development of human consciousness, as well as the shape of *SHIFT*. Transitions should be seen in their evolving, flowing movement, upward and downward, as well as backward and forward. This model for our life allows us to constantly revisit and reassess experiences that have already happened, and to draw upon those experiences for valuable information about subsequent transitions within our lives. In this way, we can proceed in life more confident that we have the necessary resources and skills, as well as the hard-earned wisdom to accomplish whatever we set out to do.

CONCLUSION

In a world moving at incredible speed, the shifts occurring in every sphere seem far more dramatic than ever before. If the future "world shifts" proposed by prominent researchers, philosophers, activists, spiritual leaders, statesman, and futurists are to become reality, and I believe they will, we're in for a pretty wild ride. But there's absolutely no reason why we can't enjoy the ride, even be exhilarated by it.

Our first goal is to take back the ownership of and responsibility for ourselves. When we do that, we can be more effective in our response to change in a way that moves us upward in the evolutionary spiral, both personally and collectively. The intention of this book is to help root you firmly in your own life while giving you the tools to creatively explore life's unlimited possibilities and potentials.

As the course of evolution spirals upward and downward, collective humanity witnesses glorious times, and horrific ones. This "need" to go to extremes, and then to course correct in order to restore balance, seems an integral function of the human psyche. Perhaps, this is an expression of the dual nature of the archetype striving to reach harmonious balance for the good of the whole.

While what we see around us globally on a daily basis may turn our stomach and make us sick with anxiety and sadness, we can attempt to see it as a course correction. Perhaps, everything that is falling apart around us is doing so for good reason; it simply has to go. Trends in recent years indicate that we are slowly returning to a more balanced state, one that had been missing for centuries. The environmental movement has centered its attention on ecology and health. An antidote to a life that has accelerated at a dizzying pace wanting more, faster, and better is the Slow Movement, which emphasizes a return to a simpler life—shedding unnecessary material goods, returning to the land, growing and eating organic foods, eco-tourism, and the like. And then there is geneaology, the study of one's roots. Individuals have a desire these days to know where they come from, who their "people" are, perhaps in a heartfelt effort to understand who they themselves are.

"The whole is more than the sum of its parts," Aristotle said in the *Metaphysics*. What this means is that it takes more than the component parts that make up a specific system to explain all of the properties of that system. Hard earned, yet ancient wisdom has taught us that it is the whole that determines how the individual parts behave, not the other way around—so much for reductionism. Let us hope that this reemerging trend toward a holistic perspective continues for a very long time.

AFTERWORD

Much of this book is about slowing down and getting more in touch with what you have within yourself already. There's so much untapped wisdom within each of us. The more you access your rich inner life, the better you understand the external life in which you find yourself. Eventually, your inner world experience has the great potential to spill over into the way you choose to live your life.

The Slow Movement describes how people are trading in their high-pressured life for one of simplicity. It's taking the "time-out" from life—the retreat, the search for quiet and solitude, minimal distractions, and being "unplugged"—up several notches.

Downshifting to Upshift Your Life

If life has gotten away from you, if the demands upon you are making you overwhelmed, anxious, depressed, and/or deeply concerned about the future, if your work-life balance is unfairly skewed away from quality time with yourself, your family, your interests and hobbies, and/or your community, then downshifting may be something to consider. *The idea is to downshift wherever and whatever you can, to streamline your life, in order to upshift the overall quality of your life.*

Of course, the practical matters of career and finances must be carefully considered in order to allow for a balanced view, since optimism about an idyllic life can carry you far away. Consider these points: Can you cut back on your hours at work? Can you work closer to home, or even from home? Can you change careers by going back to school to retrain? Can you cut back on unnecessary expenses? Can you consolidate the necessary expenses you have? What will it take to live more simply, more frugally, without compromising necessary future expenses such as children's college education, health costs, or your retirement?

If the thought of this is too overwhelming to digest all at once, simplify the exercise by creating just two categories. First, identify your **highest priorities**, those things absolutely essential for you to keep. Now, eliminate what is left. See how easy that was?

If you want to explore this further, here are some things to think about and answer for yourself.

- What are the things you value the most about your life? Choose five of these as a starting point, a basic model around which to structure the life you are trying to create.
- What commitments are most important to you? Seriously evaluate which ones are in keeping with the five things you identified as most important to you? Think about completing

your existing commitments and refusing to take on any new ones.

- Assess the way you use your time. Most of us have a daily routine, with many fixed activities and chores. Evaluate which things are absolutely necessary and important for the five areas you identified as having the most value for your life.

- How much time do you spend communicating? Assess the amount of time spent online, emailing, text messaging, and on your cell phone. How can you cut back on the amount of time you spend doing these activities? Again, it's about high priorities.

- Assess how much time you spend on a daily basis with TV, radio, the Internet, newspapers, and magazines. Decrease your consumption to receive basic information from a worthy source, *once*. So much of what is presented in the media is repetitive and redundant.

- Get rid of clutter in every area of your life. Do you really need everything you have? Give anything away you have not used in the last two years. Someone's junk is someone else's treasure. Learn to do with less.

- Assess how much quality time you actually spend with family and close friends. This will probably be one of the five things you identified as most important to you. Spend more time with someone important to you on a daily basis.

- Assess how much time you regularly make for yourself. Make time to be alone. Do what you love. Take care of yourself. Hopefully, this book has helped to make you present for your life.

RECOMMENDED READING

Adrienne, Carol. *When Life Changes or You Wish It Would: How to Survive and Thrive in Uncertain Times.* New York: HarperCollins, 2002.

Artress, Lauren. *Walking a Sacred Path: Rediscovering the Labyrinth as a Spiritual Tool.* New York: Riverhead Books, 1995.

Benson, Herbert. *The Relaxation Response.* New York: Harper Collins, 2000.

Borysenko, Joan and Gordon Dveirin. *Saying Yes to Change: Essential Wisdom for Your Journey.* Carlsbad, California: Hay House, 2005.

Braden, Gregg. *The Divine Matrix: Bridging Time, Space, Miracles, and Beliefs.* Carlsbad, California: Hay House, 2007.

———*The Spontaneous Healing of Belief: Shattering the Paradigm of False Limits.* Carlsbad, California: Hay House, 2008.

Bridges, William. *Transitions: Making Sense of Life's Changes,* Da Capo Press, 2nd edition. 2004

————*The Way of Transition: Embracing Life's Most Difficult Moments.* Cambridge, Massachusetts: Perseus Publishing, 2001

Christie, Nancy. The Gifts of Change, Hillsboro, Oregon: Atria Books/Beyond Words, 2004

Dychtwald, Ken. *Bodymind.* New York: Jeremy P. Tarcher, Inc., 1977, 1986.

Eliade, Mircea. *Rites and Symbols of Initiation.* Woodstock, Connecticut: Spring Publications, 1958.

————*The Sacred and the Profane.* New York: Harper & Row, Publishers, 1959.

Erikson, Erik. *Identity and the Life Cycle,* New York: W.W. Norton & Co., 1994.

————*The Life Cycle Completed.* New York: W.W. Norton & Co., 1998.

Gawain, Shakti. *Creative Visualization: Use the Power of Your Imagination to Create What You Want in Your Life.* New York: Bantam, 1997.

Golan, Naomi. *Passing through Transitions.* New York: Free Press, 1983.

Hubble, Mark A., Barry L. Duncan, and Scott D., Miller, eds. *The Heart and Soul of Change: What Works in Therapy*. Washington, D.C.: American Psychological Association, 1999.

Lao Tzu. *Tao Te Ching*, Baltimore, Maryland: Penguin Books, 1963

Laszlo, Ervin. *Worldshift 2012*, Rochester, Vt.: Inner Traditions, 2009.

Levinson, Daniel J., Charlotte N. Darrow, Edward B. Klein, Maria H. Levinson, and Braxton McKee. *The Seasons of a Man's Life*, New York: Ballantine Books, 1978.

Levinson, Daniel J. *The Seasons of a Woman's Life*, New York: Ballantine Books, 1996.

Lilly, John C. *The Center of the Cyclone: Looking into Inner Space*, Oakland, CA: Ronin Publishing, Inc., 1972.

————*Programming the Human BioComputer*, Oakland, CA: Ronin Publishing, 2004.

Lipton, Bruce. *The Biology of Belief: Unleashing the Power of Consciousness, Matter, and Miracles*. San Rafael, CA: Mountain of Love Productions, Inc. and Elite Books, 2005.

Neeld, Elizabeth Harper. *Tough Transitions: Navigating Your Way through Difficult Times.* New York: Warner Books, 2005.

Prochaska, James O., John Norcross, and Carlo DiClemente. *Changing for Good: A Revolutionary Six-Stage Program for Overcoming Bad Habits and Moving Your Life Positively Forward.* New York: Harper Paperbooks, 1995.

Purce, Jill. *The Mystic Spiral: Journey of the Soul.* New York: Thames and Hudson, 1974.

Ranck, Christine, and Christopher Lee Nutter. *Ignite the Genius Within: Discover Your Full Potential.* New York: Dutton, 2009.

Sheehy, Gail. *Passages.* New York: Ballantine Books, 2006.

————*New Passages.* New York: Ballantine Books, 1995.

————*Understanding Men's Passages: Discovering the New Map of Men's Lives.* New York: Ballantine Books, 1998.

Shlain, Leonard. *The Alphabet versus the Goddess: The Conflict between Word and Image.* New York: Penguin/Compass, 1998.

Spence, Sabina A. and John D. Adams. *Life Changes: A Guide to the Seven Stages of Personal Growth*. New York: Paraview, 2003.

Van Gennep, Arnold. *The Rites of Passage*. Chicago: The University of Chicago Press, 1960.

Wall, Kathleen, and Gary Ferguson. *Rites of Passage*, Hillsboro, Oregon: Beyond Words Publishing, Inc., 1998.

Wilber, Ken. *The Spectrum of Consciousness*. Wheaton, Illinois: Quest Books, 1993.

————*A Theory of Everything*. Boston: Shambhala, 2000.

Williamson, Marianne. *The Gift of Change: Spiritual Guidance for a Radically New Life*. San Francisco, CA: Harper San Francisco, 2004.

Wise, Anna. *Awakening the Mind: A Guide to Mastering the Power of Your Brain Waves*, New York: Jeremy P. Tarcher/Penguin, 2002.

————*The High Performance Mind*. New York: Jeremy P. Tarcher/Penguin, 2004.

ABOUT THE AUTHOR

Abigail Brenner, MD attended New York Medical College, becoming a physician in 1977. She completed her internship and residency in psychiatry at New York University-Bellevue Medical Center in 1981. Dr. Brenner is a board certified psychiatrist and a Fellow of the American Psychiatric Association. She is an ordained interfaith minister and a Reiki master. Dr Brenner lives and works in New York City and San Francisco.

Visit her website: www.abigailbrenner.com